CREATIVE QUESTS

Dec 2010

Published by Berryman Books

Compiled by Stephanie Innes

I am blessed to have so many inspiring creative friends and family in my life and I am honoured to be able to share their creative quests. Thank-you to all of you who have contributed, you feed my spirit in so many ways.

June 1, 2011

Dear Amber,
Wishing you joy and sunshine on your birthday and always.
Love, Shasta

CREATIVE QUESTS

Compiled by Stephanie Innes

© **2010 by** Stephanie Innes

All Rights Reserved.

No part of the printed version of this publication may be reproduced, stored in a retrieval system, or transmitted in any form or by any means, electronic, mechanical, photocopying, recording, scanning, or otherwise, except as permitted under Section 107 or 108 of the 1976 United States Copyright Act, without prior written permission of the Publisher.

ISBN 978-0-9866421-2-8

TABLE OF CONTENTS

Who needs poetry 5
If I could only have one Kiss 6
International Women's Day 1970 8
Love Plays Tricks 12
Love without limits 14
Good Loving 15
This love will carry them 18
Post-It Note for the Listener 19
Shaggy Dog Tale 21
Two Experiences of Summer 26
Autumn 29
Plant 30
MC's all over are looking for direction 34
Simply trust 35
Two Faces of Kenya 36
Brindled Silence 39
Love Poem to An Evergreen 42
The Draughtman's Contract 45

Creative Quests

Mavi (Blue) 47
Come Dance With Me 49
November Morning 51
Wise Men 53
The Edge 55
Freedom 55 58
If you dance, let it open you up 60
As a matter of fact I don't want to go back 61
Riptide 63
Mother and Son Journey to Afghanistan 65
Angelina's Triangle 68
On Grieving 70
The struggles in my life today don't even compare 71
On the Death of My Mother June 2003 74
I Fly. I Write. I Fly. 78
I pray 80

WHO NEEDS POETRY

Who needs poetry
when the waves caress the shore
with a lover's touch

Who needs poetry
when my love and I have sat on this beach all afternoon and evening
surrounded by sun & rain, clouds & campfire smoke,
rainbows & salmon peach sunset

Who needs poetry
when the cloud strewn moon
dangles in the branches of the dying arbutus
stark against the twilit sky

Who needs poetry
when this visual feast is accompanied
by the duet of upside down supper dishes laid out on a log
resonating with random plink-plonks and drip-drops
from the rain kissed trees

Who needs poetry when all the world becomes a poem……..

~ Shasta
June 27, 2009

IF I COULD ONLY HAVE ONE KISS

If I could only have one kiss
it would gently close your eyelids and
allow your inner eyes to see
that there is no horizon on the vast plains of my love
it would whisper in your innermost ear
that you are as beautiful as the stars dancing the night sky.

It would moisten the ache
below your navel and raise the hair
on the back of your neck as if the sun
had just risen after one hundred years of loneliness.
It would spark, kindle and waft the smoke of yearning
into nostrils of your deepest and most secret place.

It would taste like the memory
that first stirred the tongue to explore
beyond the teeth and lips
to that place of questioning warmth and strangeness
so unlike any other world.

If I could only have one kiss
it would never end
Just like this poetry goes on forever,
tumbling through time and space
disguised as words,
fading out into the heartbeat of silence
and the illumination of darkness.

~ Brian Hoover

Creative Quests

© David Innes . www.davinphoto.com

INTERNATIONAL WOMEN'S DAY 1970

I could have run away with you
in that moment years ago
on the curb at one a.m.
evening spent thrillingly
pasting stickers about Exploitation
all over town

remember that guy
parked at the Playboy Club
what a set-up:
we smacked one on his windshield
phallic little Porsche
he couldn't decide whether
 to call the cops or cry.

I saw us clutch our babies' hands
husbands bewildered in the doorway
the sentence for all misogyny
upon their boyish shoulders
stepping out with you
uncharted terrain
unthinkable
unconscionable
tantalizing.

oh, the devastating naughtiness
of what we could have done

I would have run away
with you because
that night we were
the Women's Movement
that night surpassed
all inklings of passion
I had ever known

    * * *

now here we are
on this dark curb
laughter as we're parting
evening trading bites upon our plates,
stories weaving shawls
gleaning little truths
no longer expecting to find
one big one.

your lover waits for you
soaking pinkly in the bath
you'll kiss her soapy breast
bobbing on wet bubbles

I'll touch my lover's temple
silver hair upon the pillow
curl my body round
his sinewed limbs

I might have run away with you
in that chilling, fevered time

Creative Quests

encountered chaos
conjured bliss
we never really chose
sidestepped
some mortal pain
and lost ... who knows
to wind up here
upon this curb
last laughter
one last kiss
date chosen when
we'll meet again.

~ Mary Anne Paré

Creative Quests

© Alan Jacques . 2 & 2

LOVE PLAYS TRICKS

Love plays tricks. It sneaks behind cupboard doors, hides underneath cabinets, gets dusty and faded. Love dissolves like disappearing ink, and turns up in flowerbeds, in neighbour's hellos, and in a pheasant's wide sweep of the sky. Love lingers, peers out of gable windows, writes notes of compassion, and knits wool socks. Love is warm, sloppy kisses, and it sometimes says, "Piss-off, you moron". Love is squirreled away in tight fisted nuts. Love is dandelion seeds parachuted across the valley. Love is listening so closely you don't notice your breath has stopped. Love is open, it's closed, it's euphoric, it's tumultuous, it's devoted, it's dazzling and mind numbing. It is twisted with complications and glows like the stars. Love plays jokes. It lingers between the bed sheets, rains in the shower stall, cooks eggs for breakfast, and pays attention to everything. It slips along the driveway and down the street, and emerges again in the grocery store, laughs at foibles, gets smitten with the universe, gets sliced open on the train tracks, and arrives home weary but willing. Love is piercing. It pokes into forbidden emotional territory. It penetrates vulnerable places. It badgers and needles. It softens and says, "I need you", or "I'm sorry." It whispers, shivers, peppers the air with bullets, goes out on Halloween and scares children. Oops. It slides underneath doors and slips out of chimneys. Love perches on treetops and takes in the view. It oozes. Squeezes. Sneezes. Upchucks. It is sickly and deadly. It lingers. It hovers. It climbs mountains. It never rests. It holds hands, sings lullabies, makes tea, feeds the dog, tells stories, bathes the children and falls asleep in the easy chair. Love is elusive, territorial, vindictive and tough. Love hides in the empty basement and emerges, unexpectedly jubilant. Love feeds the homeless, shelters the ill, crosses all borders and lines, all roadways. Love is east, west, north and south, but sometimes hides for days, even years. Love folds laundry, has a bath, and sings a new song with the volume on high. Love lurks in the shadows of the forest and howls. Love is not charming or cute. It is not fluffy. It is big and bold and boundless. It is a stallion, a dragonfly, a snake charmer. It is ancient and newborn, withheld and freely given. It is wild and tender. Love opens doors and says, "Welcome home," after a long absence, and says, "I hear you," even when words are not spoken. Love is my deepest prayer.

~ Chris Mann

LOVE WITHOUT LIMITS

My lover loves me completely
And without question
He demands nothing
And offers only love
While I love him wildly
And passionately
And make all kinds of ludicrous demands
Which he complies with
Because he loves me
So completely
He asks nothing of me
While I ask so much
Of the both of us
I bask in the way he loves me
A sweet steady undemanding love
That offers everything
And promises endurance
He finds me beautiful first thing
In the morning
And when my face
Is streaked with tears
He is teaching me how to love
Without limits
And I am both grateful
And blessed
His willing student, his lucky lover

~ Stephanie Innes
February, 2010

GOOD LOVING

Throw out the Kama Sutra
and all those Hollywood magazines
there is no manual of instructions
for your two bodies

love your own body
and you will have hot sex
allow for tenderness
and you will touch the sacred
good loving can give you this

take your parents' histories with a grain of salt
they didn't listen to their parents
and your children won't listen to you
but remember their stories
parents have gifts for you
you get to choose which ones you want to keep

forget Freud's idea
about six people in the marriage bed
there's more
the children you were
are there
between the sheets
they bring their playful sides
they bring their angry, yearning sides
no one gets to have a perfect childhood
good loving is your second chance

Creative Quests

don't look for what you think
you're missing in your other
it's there
in you
talk to yourself
locate those shadow places
tell each other what you find
you will need new language
the more you talk, the better you talk

never mind listening to me
listen to each other
embrace embrace
you are wed
  you are hitched
   you are mated
    you have Good Loving

let's dance to celebrate this joy

~ Marry Anne Paré
(This poem was written for Jessica and Joe, who work in the film industry in Los Angeles, in celebration of their wedding. Since I was officiating at this ceremony, I chose to call myself Marry Anne for the occasion.)

Creative Quests

© David Innes . www.davinphoto.com

THIS LOVE WILL CARRY THEM

He loves her more than basketball
Which he has loved deeply from the time
He could walk
She loves him more than shopping
Which she has loved passionately
Since the time she could talk
They love each other as wildly
As a prairie wind in winter
They bicker and battle
And every word is
Drenched in love
They laugh their way though every joy and challenge
Together they are more themselves
And their life is more beautiful
And everything is more possible
Because they have carried this great love
Into each other and into the world
With a fierce faith that it will carry them
Through all the pleasures and gifts, sorrows and trials,
Wonders and worries that life will bring
This love will carry them

~ Stephanie Innes
(written for Daniel and Jillian Innes for their wedding)

POST-IT NOTE FOR THE LISTENER

When you listen to me,
truly listen,
though my words are
buried in mud
within the hurricane of anguish,
and my voice is jagged, raw,
as letters spill from my mouth
like cutlery
falling down the stairs,
I feel held.

When you listen to me,
you catch me off guard,
surprise me.
You hold me with your eyes.
I am aware of each breath
of yours, of mine,
    of the hammock of kindness we rock in,
    the trust in the rope,
    the tree,
    and the hands that wove
    this net.

~ Chris Mann

© Alan Jacques . Librairie

SHAGGY DOG TALE

Once I had a shaggy dog
that reclined upon my bed
pink it was, with satin bow
on a chenille bedspread of red
its paws were tucked beneath its chin
its eyes of glass a baby blue
with stubbly tail, broad furry back,
and floppy ears that never grew.

I called my pet Delilah:
when I was young and green
she owned my heart, my secrets too
of all my pets she was the queen
but love for my stuffed puppy
transformed at age fifteen.

My ritual in early years:
I tucked us into bed
my arms curled round Delilah
on the pillow our two heads
in velvet dark we'd whisper
our dreams and our desires
my soul was hers, and hers was mine
in winter snows and summer fires.

Then one day came new yearnings
as I lay beneath my quilt
a flush crept over my body
and in my limbs I felt
a wish to hold and to be held,
a warmth between my thighs

Creative Quests

and from my hungry mouth
came startling moans and sighs

a wondrous sense was born that day
of a cavern deep inside me
a mystery cave, a lovely space,
a place of ecstacy.
well Delilah on my pillow
gazed fondly with glass eyes
when suddenly without a word
I clinched her with my thighs

I rode my shaggy dog
like a steed, a mount, a beast,
and all the love I felt for her
enhanced my body's feast
while in my mind there came
 to my utmost surprise
 the image of a grade ten boy
skinny, tall, with dark brown eyes

They say the first time's special
Well, that day was just the start
I found the body's union
with mind and soul and heart
so many explorations
for Delilah and for me
but the oath till death do us two part
 was not for us to be
*

My social life took off
by the time I reached sixteen
I wanted, like my girlfriends,
to hit the party scene
along with music and with dance
came the flow of alcohol
ah, Bacchus filled my throat
and that was my downfall.

It was in the early hours
I stumbled to my bed
Where, there upon my pillow
oh the shame, the pain, the dread
Delilah, in her innocence
lay paws tucked under chin
when I stretched out beside her
my head began to spin

And all the churning contents
of my brewing belly spewed
over my sweet shaggy pup
oh it was vulgar, it was lewd
the sight of that dear doggy
barf matting fur dull pink
bits of vomit in her floppy ears
it was enough to swear off drink

Well learn I did in time
to imbibe and hold my own
but too late, too late Delilah
as my story has now shown

that was the end of childhood
dear companion left behind
her resting place no pillow now
she lives fondly in my mind

I have had many happy days
 of love and many splendoured nights
what I recall and cherish still
are my shaggy dog's delights
I learned to trust and love my body
I'll keep that till life's end
and know a shaggy pink stuffed dog
can be a girl's best friend.

~ Mary Anne Pare wrote this poem as an entry for a Vagina Monologues performance. The poem won and was performed on Pender Island!

© David Innes . Early Dawn . www.davinphoto.com

TWO EXPERIENCES OF SUMMER

Summer Delight

I float on the water
feeling its smooth,
rippling, velvety coolness -
a very sexual caress.
I open myself to the sensation
that makes all pain,
all heartache retreat.
Seaweed flutters beneath.
Tiny fish nibble at my toes.
Purple anemones cluster in the depth.
I am alone under the vast blue sky.
I stretch my arms wide, arch my back,
basking in the sun's rays above
but cold with goosebumps underneath.
This grace is all I need to feel
every atom in me fully alive.

Summer Heat

It enfolds me, this summer heat.
Fondles leaves, grass, and loamy soil.
They spread, stretch, steam,
giving off their special scent.

I breathe deep, suck it down
and feel the warmth within.
Feel all that August energy
from sun, sand and ocean.

The touch of fiery beams
upon my naked skin.
The caress of salty brine.
Aroma of pungent kelp.

Summer times to be lazy –
relaxing and opening to the sun.
Drinking in all nature.
Letting go in order to grow.

Too hot? Too crowded? Too busy?
No – just be still.
Be quiet, slow the blood.
Be, just be - rooted, centered.

Glorious season of freedom!
Unrestrained by walls or muffling clothes.
I open, embracing, glowing,
changing, imbibing life.

~ Barbara Matiru

© Barbara Matiru

AUTUMN

golden tree
one by one
your slender arms remove
with the wind's
assistance
your trembling gown

whole forests
drape their skirts
on the green
hillsides

night comes sooner
and with it
blown amber stars.

~ Calvin Rambler

PLANT

we know not
   where our illness comes from
we fortunate citizens of
 these so-called
   developed nations.

we see not
  as we race along
that we are sick
in our core
ailing
in this land that ranks
foremost
 in quality
    of life

rush hour life styles
eyes
  on the computer screen
hands
  on the steering wheel
 backs turned
   on the hands
    that tend the soil

we have lost
  the most beloved
we have lost
  our kinship

with the Mother
with the earth.

forsaken
   our belonging
   to the land

proceed as if
it belongs to us
dump spray pump
for our necessities
coffee, tobacco, oil
crops out of sight
   wrung from the soil
      grace our tables
         please our palates

our desire is
   whatever we can pay for

estranged
from ground
tilled by forefathers
gardened by foremothers
shun the family farm
pander the corporate
banish the fecund fields
urban environs sealing
   the soil
   that feeds us all
   that keeps heart
   and mind

Creative Quests

  and hand
    in balance
the soil that is
    the dust
      that is
        us.

*   *   *   *   *

Take
This flat oval
seed
Raised ridge along
its outer rim
place it
in the earth

sun comes
 rain falls
days lengthen
the planet breathes
 in early autumn
stop
along the garden path
see
this plump bright pumpkin
Sitting in its leafy nest

remember
  then
    the miracle

drop
  by the wayside
  fill up
  with
    quiet joy

~ Mary Anne Paré

© David Innes . Jolly Roger . www.davinphoto.com

Creative Quests

MC's all over are looking for direction
The answer to the question is truly introspection
"When you know who you are, then you'll know what to say,
And when you say it, say it in your very own way"
These were the words of a man that I once knew
I went forth with his wisdom and this is how I do
It ain't nothin' new, but he said stay true
I listened real close and its gotten me through
Some of the toughest times, some of the dopest rhymes
The best of friends who decided to drop dimes
Matter fact, let me just speak on "friends"
Speak on those who cared more about ends
The pain still lingers and I'll never make amends
You all ride to the top and then it descends
In the end it's all really confusing
And it never would've stopped until I went and stopped the using

~ Daniel Innes

SIMPLY TRUST

Don't the leaves
flutter down
Just like that
Such simple beauty
In an ancient Japanese Haiku
Such gentle wisdom
Simply trust
We westerners
Clutter everything up
With flowery phrases
And pretty poetry
Alluring alliteration
Obscuring the wisdom
Waiting to be revealed
Simply trust

~ Stephanie Innes

TWO FACES OF KENYA

Early Morning in Naro Moro
Such exquisite coolness,
after the scorching day,
and humid, restless night!
I drink it in, breathe
deeply of the piney scent
wafted through my window
on a gentle breeze.
I stretch to meet its
dewy freshness,
relishing the goose bumps
on my bare skin.

My eyes feast on
wave after wave of
mist-encircled mountains.
Silver veils rise
from their valleys,
tinged in pink,
as the sun begins
its daily journey.

The trout stream
gurgles nearby.
A tawny gazelle
sips sweet water
in a back eddy.
Above, in the canopy,

A vervet monkey
peeks curiously down.
Is that an elephant
swaying through the trees?
Oh, gentle time of
birdsong praises,
pearl-decked leaves,
earthy scents,
with me, the
only one awake.

Drought in Turkana
Small, brown,
listless toddlers
squatting on
the parched earth.

Ribs so prominent,
potbellies a lie
of good nourishment.
Faces streaked with dirt,
nostrils crusted,
lips cracked,
eyes drinking pools
for countless flies.

No strength to
Brush them away.

~ Barbara Matiru

Creative Quests

© Barbara Matiru . Mt. Kenya

BRINDLED SILENCE

Many-eyed beech with your woodholes
and mouths, speak
to me of whiteness and the cold winter come.

How it ravens
through the trees! Alters, skeins
the brackish pools with solder.

Branched elder
paperysoft unbundles in your loftiness, reaches
down
to trammel insects' lairs.

Trunk riddled brown; as if
a hundred hungry moths eating away
at your scrolls
had hardened and become part of you.

Breezy winter harbinger
staggered from the fold -- why do you
stand alone?
Struck-lightning white against a canopy of conifers.

Branches bowed
against blue nothingness. Glimpsed through a window in passing
you are emblazoned,
etched sharply as a guncrack under sky,
its starred
entry a wound to the household.
*

Summer has fled, frittered away by your boughs,
your stretched pale
fingers upholding Autumn's crown.

Bold outlier, snowy warder,
keep the woods from encroaching. At least until
their needles
(a staggered silvery of swords) have rusted
and coppered your roots.

Hold in your arms
the weakened sun, stripped of its embers
and beamglare.
Paint these magesterial trees, Lord, but let the beech
stand
for what remains unfinished, its peeling pages
forever unread.

~ Calvin Rambler

Creative Quests

© Lia McCormick

LOVE POEM TO AN EVERGREEN

Oh to be a dancing green tree
on a bright blue day in early spring

Oh the joy of your dance
in the cool morning breeze
as you open to the fiery kiss of the sun
spreading slowly down the length
of your sturdy brown body
radiating warmth and life
to the very tips of your graceful green limbs
all the way down to your roots
in the moist fecund earth

Oh the miracle of your roots
how they spiral and snake through the ground
branching endlessly into ever thinner strands
weaving themselves into the glorious subterranean
tapestry of microbes and mycelia
the vast and unseen network
by which you draw nourishment from the very elements
of this molten earth
over which we stumble through our daily lives
all unknowing

Ah but you know
in way that's I never will
how it feels to be on such intimate terms
with the touch of the sun
the caress of the breeze
the kiss of the rain

*

You know how to fully and effortlessly
inhabit the space
around you
above you
below you

You know how it feels
to never have your umbilical cord severed
to never have to leave your mother
rather to sense yourself
growing deeper into her
every day you are alive

And even when you grow old and die
as does everything eventually
(even this earth, even this sun, perhaps even this universe)
even then your dance goes on

You lie in state on the forest floor
feeding generation after generation
of saplings
of creatures who fly and creep and nest
of eyes that hunger for meaning and wonder
and find it in you
in all your stages of life and death

Oh to be a dancing green tree
on a bright blue day
in early spring

~ Shasta
February 2005

Creative Quests

© Shasta

THE DRAUGHTMAN'S CONTRACT

Come, whisper your tales into my open pages.
Tell me where it was they came to you,
Four-legged in the dark.

That low flame only touches ground when bells sing.

Piece these ruins out of the past, plait them for me.
Pull them golden through your fingers, please.
Wash the sun from their long strands.

I will sit with nightjars till the mad stars ring.

Foot-of-the-tree pools stretched dark at its base.
Tell me, teach me. Thirst these gardens down
Hedgerows the draughtsman drew.

This parchment wants words, not images.

Crib your notes. That distant ridge will not hold.
Lines lie, draughtsmen succomb, the summer heat
Shall rise to balloon you. Pare your slender instrument.

There is an art to conversation.

Curves hold silences redder than the sun.
Apocalypse me, now. Pour your voice
Into the chalice, outheld, that swirls conviction.

~ Calvin Rambler

© Chris Mann . Helen's violin

MAVI (BLUE)

Today, at this moment
I am the shine of ink
on a note of farewell.

I blinked, closing my eyes
for a single heartbeat,
and the blue-skinned djinn
that had suffered to be held

Like smoke in the lungs,
like water cupped for drinking

Evaporated, dissolved,
turned and shimmered
before my open fingers

Emptied, suddenly,
of what I had held
dear, so close

For the space
of a heartbeat

Thinking it was mine.

~ Calvin Rambler

© Lia McCormick

COME DANCE WITH ME

I am a rock at the tideline of the ocean of your imagination.
I am as jagged and craggy or as smooth and round
as your curiosity will allow.
This rock, without you the listener, is but a word without a story,
somehow left by the wayside, meaningless,
without longing or life.

This rock rests in a lap of sand as the tide comes in.
Wave upon wave approaches, getting closer.
On some days the waves crash and roar and on others
they bring a gentle kiss.
But every day, dancing to the song of the moon, they advance.
At first there is a gentle touch of moisture
which surrounds the rock, then it is submerged in another world.
Currents of air are replaced by currents of water,
bringing all manner of creation, some of it alive and seeking,
some of it dead – being given by the ocean as if it were
some strange gift to the land.

Each wave brings a new pulse and note, creating a song, until
the moon calls the ocean back, the fish vanish, and slowly
the waves retreat.

The rock is exposed to air once again as the larger pulse
of high tide and low tide fulfils its own cycle.
During this journey the rock has been ever so slightly eroded
by the very sand it rests in, becoming the sand
that will continue to erode the rock until finally,
there is nothing but sand,
singing other rocks into a gritty oblivion.

Creative Quests

So as the journey of the tide with its long slow pulse
and ever changing wave patterns ebbs and flows,
so then our own journeys have pulse and pattern, taking us apart,
reshaping us, and including us in a dance we come to willingly or not.

I am a rock at the tideline of the ocean of your imagination.
Come, dance with me.

~ Brian Hoover
Still Meadow, March 2007

© Jacques Alan . Arc

NOVEMBER MORNING

Today our new house on the hill
wakes up in a swirl of restless fog
defies us to remember
our view of mountains, of sky.

We dust fading dreams
from our shoulders
and touch warm skin
under purple sheets.

This bitter November morning
is awash in mist and mystery,
the lamp posts glow orange still,
in Narnian expectation
beyond the wardrobe of our limitations.

Once, a white tailed hawk
swung low over the grasslands in our valley,
and we could see beyond
the trees circling the lake
to mountain after mountain after mountain.

Every grass, leaf and feather
was etched in precision
against a perfect summer sky.

Today we nestle in the mist
which cloaks our autumn morning,
content to see nothing
and feel everything.

~ Chris Mann

Creative Quests

© Chris Mann . Bleeding Hearts

WISE MEN

Drunks, in the lee of a bus booth
Open to the weather
Rasping, with accoustic strains
What wise men know:
Only fools rush in.

The old chestnut
Roasted,
In their rendition,
By lyrics forgotten
Over the years.

I
can't
help
falling in love
With
These voices.

Only a fool could
Stand in the first storm of winter
Unmoved by the fury
Of faces
Lit by fond remembrance.

Love is never lost, I read
In their rubied cheeks, emblazoned
With cold. It merely falters.
And joy, proclaim the wise,
Three liquored harlots for a choir

Is seldom lessened for its lack;
Especially when cups
Burned clean of honey-mead
Chill
The singer's fingers.

~ Calvin Rambler

© Chris Mann . Monarch

THE EDGE

As I walk along the edge
of the canyon carved by
the river of my life
I look down
I hear the river below
singing with the sun above
I see the layers of rock
telling their own still story
I touch the edge and feel it's keen danger
I touch the dampness of decay
and the freshness of this moment

I stop and sit on this edge.
There are a million unsung
songs waiting to be given a voice
my voice, I'll get to a few of them

I wait and I breathe
taking it all in
sitting in wonder at the
sheer improbability of all this
and the unstoppable momentum
bearing down on it with the
weight of the stars behind it

I look up the canyon
toward the source,
long ago lost to plain view,
my gratitude is deep.

Creative Quests

Such effort has been made
to get me to this point
and yet effort freely given.

I look down the canyon
toward the unseen sea
to which all rivers flow,
mystery lies that way
and I walk towards it with wonder
dizzying, stupefying,
in anticipation of the songs
to be sung and the stories to be told.

I like this edge place
it is uncomfortable
although my visit here is brief
my spirit is recharged
reminded of it's place
among the stars
and of the infinite web
of which I am this momentary spinner

~Brian Hoover

Creative Quests

© Lia McCormick

57

Creative Quests

FREEDOM 55

Happy Birthday my beloved Brian.
Like so many of your fellow baby boomers
you are 55 and free.
Unlike so many of your fellow baby boomers
your "Freedom 55" does not constitute early retirement
from a job you never much liked anyway.
Instead, your Freedom 55 consists of the conscious choice
to joyously continue the work you love,
are brilliant at and perfectly suited for,
knowing that you and the instruments you craft
grow ever more valuable
as you grow older, wiser and more experienced.

Your Freedom 55 entails buying a third set of conga drums,
these ones antiques in need of some TLC which only one
with skills such as yours can provide.
Not that you bought them just for the challenge of fixing them
up.
No, you bought them because they have that particularly Cuban sound
you've worked so diligently to achieve
for these past five years,
ever since we took up studying with a Latin madman.
You can bet he won't be retiring at 55 either.

Your Freedom 55 allow you the time and space
to get together with two of your best friends,
one a Jew, the other a Sufi Muslim,
to sing, dance and read ecstatic poetry to each other.

I recall the plan you had cooked up
for the three of you to "get drunk on Rumi and Hafiz
and go reeling from door to door shouting 'I love you!' into the night".
Now that's what I call freedom.

My sweet love, lover and beloved
on this day, after 55 years of walking through this life
you are as free as you have ever been.
I know, however, that it is a hard-won freedom.
For much of your earlier life you had to do battle
with the little grey men who invaded your temple
and told you all manner of lies about yourself,
about this life and your place in it.
I'm happy to say it very much appears that at this point in your life
you've got them on the run.

What a great honour and joy it is for me
to witness and take part in your ongoing process
of disentanglement from the sticky web of deception
called "appropriate behaviour" or "acting your age".
Here's wishing you many more decades of
outrageousness, impropriety and, of course, freedom.
On you it looks good.

~ Shasta
June 27, 2004

Creative Quests

If you dance, let it open you up. If you write, let it fill you and spill over into the hearts of those who read what you have written. Let the world move through you and embrace you so you feel its heat and let it pierce you with its cold. Stand in the centre of the weather without shrinking back from the wind, the rain, the heat, the storm. Let yourself be touched by life. Live at the centre of it. Even if it's occasionally terrifying or excruciating, it's worth it. Because it is often exhilarating, liberating and wildly fulfilling there in the centre of your life. Stay there, in the face of all that comes to confront you. Meet what comes with grace, embrace it with wonder. Whatever it is – a newfound love, an amazing trip, a dying mother, a deep longing – it is all yours. Here to be experienced – to be lived fully. Live it all at the centre, gently, gracefully. You do not have to be devoured by it, nor do you have to battle it, you only have to let the soft underbelly of your heart open to all that it feels. Surrender. Gracefully. Trust. Breathe in with ease. It will all come together. With you, right there at the centre of it. If at times you need shelter from the storm that surrounds you, allow yourself a gentle space – don't let the storm batter you. Give over to it and feel the wind embrace you and the rain caress you. Feel the wild exhilaration of the wind throwing the cold rain onto your hot skin. And if you are drenched and damp and exhausted, give in to yourself. Open up an umbrella and delight in the reprieve before you return to that wild raw place you have claimed at the centre of your life.

~ Stephanie Innes

As a matter of fact I don't want to go back
Could do with a change I like my mental intact
There's been doubts raised and they've all been contended
Messages were sent incompletely and blended
What was done by one is really what ten did
Hindsight is 20/20 now isn't that splendid
Regrets coupled with shame and despair
A plight like my own could never compare
A forgotten life was the trap and I fell for the snare
In the patchwork of life I could feel a tear
"Stop" I screamed but the words reside on the inside
Externally I exhibit the wounds of each time I lied
At the point where I am avoided like a pesticide
With plenty to hide, I can't let it slide,
I am not at the "ex" so get me off this ride
The realization of choice climbs in slowly
Searching for a way that is no longer lowly
Done with being holy, rolling with the only
just walking my path and looking for the whole me

~ Daniel Innes

© Barbara Matiru

RIPTIDE

Moving strips the tar
right off my skin,
reaches in to stir
my skeleton with a witch's broom.

Every atom of my being
is transported
to different planets,
cobbled back together
like a broken glass
on the sidewalk,
never to be the same.

I am an autumn silhouette,
a naked tree falling,
my leaves ripped from me,
my roots yanked
from the earth
in a storm of
memories, moments, madness.

I am a tangle of papers,
a jumble of pictures,
a basket of handprints,
on wet sand,
the paint and polish
licked clean with chemicals
and biting wind.

They say there is always
calm after the storm.

*
So I sit
in a room painted red
by tired arms.
I remember the love in these new walls,
and wait for the salt to evaporate
from this sting of change.

~ Chris Mann

MOTHER AND SON JOURNEY TO AFGHANISTAN

"He wants to make
 the world a better place,"
The Sun reports in its
coverage of the war.
And, there was a
photo of Charles -
gazing out at me.

Now he scans
the barren hills.
A helmet protects his head.
A webbed belt holds
grenades and gun.
He carries one of
the newest assault rifles.

He feels all this is a conceit –
false protection against death.
His eyes are never still:
searching the dreary landscape,
for non knows from where
the next attack might come.

Six of his buddies
in Charlie Company
are no more.
Their youthful bodies,
prisoners in their vehicle,
torn apart by

Creative Quests

buried bombs
while on the way
to build a village school.

"What has been
accomplished here in
these past six months?"
he ponders anew.
But, perhaps it's
not about that.
Rather, it's more
how he now views life
so very differently.

In Kandahar,
children cower in
doorways afraid.
Indeed, he is
a fearful sight
in full battlegear.
At Christmas,
Charles feels some hope,
distributing woolly caps,
to clusters of little ones
shivering in the snow.

Such a land of contrasts:
searing heat at noon,
freezing cold at night;
ancient Muslim wisdom,

today's radical fanaticism;
scattered limbs on open road,
team mates heartily slapping
each other on the back
before the next grueling tour.

And I, I pray each day
that my tall, gentle,
loving, youngest son
will return alive
to give me peace,
even if there is
no peace yet
in Afghanistan.

~ Barbara Matiru

ANGELINA'S TRIANGLE

Three sisters grieving over the passing of their parents.
First Dad then two months later, at 3: am the call comes.
 Your Mom is almost gone, Angelina's time has come.
Sisters Marilyn and Margaret hurry to catch the wave of eternity of mom's next journey, sister Merle from abroad, in spirit.
Husbands rally to their need.
She's on the third floor in the third bed clockwise from the door.
Heart's rhythm of life silent, at peace with the universe.
Three sides of her bed welcoming her daughters to say their prayers, blessings and good byes.
 One for each side of Angelina's triangle.
 Each so different yet so connected to the other.
Spirits of Norm and Ann, father and mother, the nucleolus within the centre, hover ever so softly.
She lies now so quiet, so surreal.
Three rings drawn from her still warm hands for remembrance sake.
Three times a call went out to sister Merle from beyond the hospital doors to no avail.
Thirty minutes have passed and the reality sets in that Mom's spirit has begun to drift.
 Out beyond this third rock from the sun to join her soul mate.
Returning home three kilometers to prepare the long list of friends and relatives to call.
Of course, the three favorite grandchildren at the top of the list.
Sister Merle soon to arrive for the third time in a year.
Then the triangle will be complete to reminisce one to one to one of all the times, good and bad.
Mom and Dad's spirits filling the room.

Three M's together as one, as it should be.
To grieve and celebrate the three absolutes of our humanism,
birth, life, death.
Angelina's triangle created with sweet love, strength and wisdom
will carry on.

~ Bob Timms
April 1, 2009

ON GRIEVING

You are not alone. As much as you feel like you are the only person who has ever cracked open with the depth of a grief that could not possibly be survived, I promise you, you are not alone. This is the map I offer you to navigate through a darkness with no light.

You are allowed to make mistakes. To say the wrong thing, to do the wrong thing, to feel confused and terrified and do nothing. You are allowed to be wrong. It will not kill you. You are allowed to cry, to ache, to break open with the sadness that is in you. You are allowed to let other people down to take care of yourself. You are allowed to be afraid, to feel lonely, to be hopeless and frightened and fearful. To cry for days, to grieve your losses and fall apart. You are allowed to turn off the phone and pull down the blinds and eat popcorn and watch bad movies. You are allowed to escape. To try and forget this aching pain. You are allowed to be sad, to feel it at the depths of who you are and to let it break you open and take you closer to your own centre. You are allowed to cry in public. You are allowed to not cry at all. You are allowed to want to forget and escape. To be angry. To feel sorry for yourself. You are allowed to ask people to touch you or to not touch you, to bring you food or leave you alone. You are allowed to talk incessantly about this loss, this unbearable grief. You are allowed to cry. To wail out at the unfairness of it all. To weep often and uncontrollably. Life is messy. Death is messy. You are allowed to be messy. And know that you are complete and whole and you will survive and come together again and you will be different than you were before. Closer to your centre, more raw, more real, messier. Yes, you are allowed to be messy. If you want to. You are allowed to do anything you want to right now.

You are allowed to be lost and sad and momentarily incomplete. To do what you want, when you want, how you want. You are allowed to feel your pain and your grief and your sorrow. To be angry at the world for all that you have lost, including precious parts of yourself. You are allowed to do everything wrong. To be imperfect. And still perfectly lovable. You are allowed to get lost in this grief, to feel it deeply and disappear into it. To take a sick day or two or ten.

But only temporarily because life with all its beauty, rawness and messiness is waiting. Waiting for your full attention so it can show you a stunning sunset, the northern lights, a child's giggle, a wild ocean, a branch enfolded by frost, a tulip opening in the springtime, a raindrop on a perfect spider-web. Life is waiting to show you its gentleness as well as its harshness. It is waiting for you to heal enough to open to the beauty around you. So a friend can wrap her arms around you and another can bring you a beautiful meal, a song can touch you and move you not to tears but to dancing, the smile of a stranger can fill you with a warmth you had forgotten was possible. Your life is waiting to give you one small gift after another. You can again embrace it, its beauty and its messiness, knowing it is absolutely and completely yours. Because you have survived it. Over and over, you have survived the intensity of all that your life gives you, you have dived into it, immersed yourself in it and been opened to yourself and the world around you. When you're ready, when your heart has broken open to the world, your beautiful, painful, messy life is waiting with open arms to give you all the gifts of yourself.

Walk into it, slowly, trusting life to heal you with the same love that has broken you open. Carry that love with you and hold it up to the light and when the tears come, let the tears come, and when the joy comes, let the joy come. Let it all come, let it all fall out into your centre and live your life from that centre. Because you know now, what the world can take from you, and you know also, what the world can give you. This knowing makes everything sacred. Live fully in this world with all your wisdom and your broken open heart full of love and grief and wonder. Live the sacred gifts that are yours and yours alone.

~ Stephanie Innes, 2005

© Chris Mann

The struggles in my life today don't even compare
To the life that I used to live when I was out there
On a tare without a care, how could I prepare?
I had it in my head, that life wasn't fair
But life is a choice and today that's what I choose
I've put aside the drugs and I've put aside the booze
I'm not up here preaching, I don't want to confuse
But when everyone was winning that's when I'd lose
Everyone progressed, but I regressed and stood still
Tried to get out, but I never had the will
Told myself I was in it just for the thrill
Never had a clue that I was really truly ill
I've been blessed 3600 times in the last hour
From the time I woke up to those seconds in the shower
Time is what we have-what we do with it is power
So be yourself, stay true, and as for you-never cower

~ Daniel Innes

ON THE DEATH OF MY MOTHER
JUNE 2003

now we stand
  around this empty body
that was yours
dress worn that recent family wedding
hair brushed back some style not yours
recall a story you loved telling

 your side of the family
 nephew of a cousin
 peering at the coiffed
 and powdered corpse
of great aunt Gertrude
 exclaimed
   why   I must say
    she's looking well!

so we stand
  around your empty body
refrain from saying so
but yes we think
you do indeed look well

we breathe relief together
journey's last leg eased
our caring hands
a patch of morphine on your skin
close company to see you go

*

in almost every way
I am at peace
(and yet)
you said yourself
  short days before
    such a happy death I'm having

(and yet)
there is a voice that whispers
never go, my mother, never go
now   I want to know
all I chose not to ask
hear   all you chose
not to say
see you there
at the corner of the sofa
library books crossword puzzles piled around you
waiting bright eyes for
someone to pass by

and yet and yet
another voice
uneasy truce
with fury (mine not yours)
the world you lived your life in
did not allow your rightful size
confined
   to fit the life of women
 allotted by the times

*

Creative Quests

confinement
(the nerve to call it that)
conceal the swelling belly
   oozing breasts gushing groin
semblance required to be
wife of the doctor   mother of nine

adept at diminishment
what worked for others was
what worked for you
lost sight to your   own shine

 final years
  desire gone
   not you to rage
    against
     the dying light

our breath around your deathbed
 sparked dim embers
you flickered   flared
those last days
your body was our hearth
   listen you said
let me tell you stories
  new twists to
ones I've told again again
read to me dance sing play music
feed me glorious ice cream
  caress your hands across my crumbling skin

yes... yes ...yes...lovely
your leaving blessed us
like the setting sun
how could we not be glad?

my rage smoulders
still in the ashes of your passing
I will not let it die
it fuels the life that I live now
your stories
 told untold
illuminate the passage
of my own remaining years

~ Mary Anne Paré

Creative Quests

I FLY. I WRITE. I FLY.

If I write, I will fly.
If I write fear, even fear, I will fly.
If I fly
    a ragged spiral
    a flap, thrust
    spin, wobble
        nose dive into glass...

If I fly over stories
of resistance, past
fields of unspoken,
unnamed truths...

If I circle into dizziness
and drop feathers like bombs...
Do Not Run
from me,
I will not stop,

nor rest on any branch
or resist obstacles I crunch into.

I will not succumb any more
to earth bound voices of
restraint.
I will not bind to cage or harness.

And now that I can fly
I will write,
even if my words
slip from strings like beads
and ideas toss from boats at sea.

I will retrieve them all
and cradle salty letters
and winged thoughts
and
yes,
I will write.

~ Chris Mann

I PRAY

I pray for the wisdom
To empty myself of all knowledge
So that I might learn
I pray that I am guided
To be more loving and generous
And committed to living well
I pray to be reminded
That from the darkness
The tree's roots are nourished
I pray for the strength
To be soft when faced with hardness
To open when I want to close
I pray for the courage
To walk the one path
Meant for my feet
I pray for your love
To move through me
Into this world
I pray for the ability
To recognize the face of god
In each face
And feel the warmth of your love
Spread over me like sunshine
Even on cloudy days
I pray to remember to be grateful for the simplest most important things
Things that have everything to do with love and nothing to do with money

I pray for the wisdom
To know that grace is always present

~ Stephanie Innes

© Alan Jacques . Paris